CAUSES
OF THE
COLD WAR

STEWART ROSS

HODDER
Wayland

an imprint of Hodder Children's Books

© 2001 White-Thomson Publishing Ltd

Produced for Hodder Wayland
by White-Thomson Publishing Ltd
2/3 St Andrew's Place
Lewes
BN7 1UP

Series concept: Alex Woolf
Editor: Nicola Edwards
Designer: Derek Lee
Consultant: Scott Lucas, Head of American and Canadian
  Studies, University of Birmingham.
Proofreader: Sue Lightfoot

Published in Great Britain in 2001 by Hodder Wayland, a
division of Hodder Children's Books

Map illustrations by Nick Hawken.

British Library Cataloguing in Publication Data
Ross, Stewart
  The causes. - (The Cold War)
  1. Cold War
  I. Title
  909.8'25

ISBN 0 7502 3384 2

Printed and bound in Italy by G. Canale & C.S.p.A., Turin

Hodder Children's Books
A division of Hodder Headline Limited
338 Euston Road, London NW1 3BH.

Picture acknowledgements: The publishers would like to thank
the following for giving permission to use their pictures:
Cover: (left) AKG photo; (centre) Corbis; (right) Peter
Newark; title page: Corbis; AKG photo 6, 12, 23, 25, 36,
37, 38, 42, 53, 54, 59; Camera Press 50; Corbis 43; HWPL
8, 14 © National Maritime Museum, 15 © Imperial War
Museum, 18, 19, 24 © Imperial War Museum, 31 ©
Associated Press, 44, 45, 60 (both), 61 (top) © Imperial War
Museum, 61 (bottom); Peter Newark 5, 7, 9, 13, 16, 17, 20,
22, 39, 48, 52, 55, 56, 58; Popperfoto 4, 10, 11, 27, 28, 30,
33, 34, 35, 41, 47, 49, 51, 57; Topham 26, 29, 32

Contents

CHAPTER ONE

An Age Defined

A MEETING OF ALLIES

SHORTLY AFTER mid-morning on 25 April 1945, less than a fortnight before the ending of World War II in Europe, American patrols of the Sixty-ninth Division reached the western bank of the River Elbe, Germany. On the opposite bank they spotted soldiers of the Soviet Union's Red Army, America's most powerful ally.

Signalling that they were friends, the Americans crossed the river and were greeted by the Soviets with smiles and hugs. Vodka appeared, toasts were drunk, someone produced a concertina and before long an impromptu party was in full swing to celebrate the first meeting of the allies' front lines.

▼ A carefully posed photograph of the first meeting of US and Soviet troops on 25 April 1945. The apparent warmth of their greetings was soon frozen out by the coming of the Cold War.

AN IRON CURTAIN

Reports say the young men and women (many females served in the Red Army) swore vague oaths of comradeship but were prevented by linguistic barriers from holding meaningful conversations. If this was so, then it was alarmingly significant. Like their soldiers, the US and Soviet governments expressed friendship but spoke and thought in very different languages. The Americans came from the world of liberal democracy, the Russians from the world of communism. The two were not compatible.

Only weeks after the meeting on the Elbe, the British Prime Minister Winston Churchill used a phrase he was later to make famous. He was worried, he wrote to US President Harry Truman, because the Red Army had drawn an 'iron curtain' across its front line. There would be no more toasts and dancing. Instead, America and the Soviet Union, each backed by powerful allies, drifted further apart until, by 1948, they stood at the very brink of war. There they halted and engaged in four decades of open, dangerous rivalry. This was the Cold War.

EAST AND WEST

The depth of East-West mistrust is clearly shown in these two extracts, both from 1946. The first was written by George Kennan, a US diplomat working in Moscow, the second by Nikolai Novikov, the Soviet Ambassador in Washington.

" … we have here a political force [the USSR] committed fanatically to the belief that with the US there can be no permanent modus vivendi [working together], that it is desirable and necessary that the internal harmony of our society be disrupted, our traditional way of life be destroyed, the international authority of our state be broken."

"The foreign policy of the United States, which reflects the imperialist tendencies of American monopolistic capital, is characterized in the postwar period by a striving for world supremacy."

▼ "We are very happy" reads the placard in this French anti-Soviet cartoon of 1935. Before 1941 hostility towards the communists was widespread in the Western press.

THE ARMS RACE

The phrase 'Cold War' was first used in 1947 by the US presidential advisor Bernard Baruch. He meant that hostility between the US-led 'Western' bloc and the Soviet-led 'Eastern' bloc had many of the features of a war, but stopped short of a 'hot' or shooting war. Like other wars, it involved each side building up armaments in an attempt to outstrip and overawe the other. This 'arms race' became the Cold War's most prominent feature.

▲ The Apollo 11 moon landing of 1969 showed that, after falling behind the USSR in the 1950s, the US had taken a firm lead in the space race.

A DIVIDED WORLD

As US-Soviet posturing and manipulation lay at the heart of the Cold War, it is the central theme of this book. Nevertheless, it is important to remember that other nations – for example, Britain, France, Italy, China and Czechoslovakia – played a significant role in the War's development.

As the Cold War deepened, each side sought allies. After swallowing up much of Eastern Europe, the Soviets looked for supporters further afield. Meanwhile, the US strengthened its ties with Britain and Western Europe, and built up new friendships in the Americas, Australasia and Asia. The communist takeover in China in 1949 added a new, unpredictable dimension to the tension (see page 45).

East-West rivalry also influenced lesser confrontations and conflicts. For instance, it helped shape the Arab-Israeli wars and the break up of European empires in Africa and elsewhere. In Europe itself, it was a key factor in the development of what is now the European Union.

A NEAR-TOTAL CONFLICT

Although we will concentrate primarily on diplomatic and military history, the Cold War also saw a variety of non-military strategies deployed. These included economics (see pages 22–23) and official and unofficial propaganda (see page 56). This made the Cold War almost as 'total' as the preceding World War. It distorted (and finally destroyed) the Soviet economy by diverting an exorbitant proportion of national wealth towards the military. The demands of the armed forces on both sides spurred rapid technological development too, notably in aviation and communications. The space race, a semi-military spin off from the arms race, produced orbital satellites and, in 1969, the first moon landing.

The nuclear stand-off spawned films, novels, poetry and a whole new genre of spy thrillers. In society at large it encouraged blinkered thinking, paranoia and jingoism. Even athletes were encouraged to see themselves as ambassadors of a way of life.

STABILITY THROUGH FEAR

Finally and paradoxically, it could be argued that the Cold War brought to the post-war world a stability missing since 1914. The presence of two major power blocs clarified and simplified international politics. As much by luck as judgement, the system prevented the global catastrophe of nuclear war. This was not a prediction many would have made when the Cold War began in the dark years following World War II.

SOVIET SYSTEM IS BEST

There was great admiration for the way the Red Army had defeated Nazi Germany in the east. In 1946, Joseph Stalin, the Soviet leader, claimed that this proved the superiority of what he called the 'Soviet social system':

"The war has shown that the Soviet social system is a … perfectly viable and stable form of organization of society. More than that, … the Soviet social system has proved more viable and stable than a non-Soviet social system… [and] a better form of organization of society."

▶ Joseph Dzhugashvili, commonly known simply as Stalin ('Man of Steel'), saw himself as a sort of communist tsar determined to defend the interests of his country against encircling capitalism.

CHAPTER TWO

The Roots of the Cold War

A CONFLICT OF IDEOLOGY

Unlike a 'hot' war, the Cold War did not follow a declaration of war or a sudden act of aggression. Like nightfall, it crept over the world until, by 1950, it had blotted out all that had been before. The roots of this change lay deep in the past.

Fundamentally, the Cold War was a conflict between two ideologies and the systems of government they produced. One was Western liberal democracy. This advocated rule by the people's elected representatives, and held that governments might broadly regulate the economy but should leave its day-to-day operation to the free market. The other, at the heart of the Soviet and, later, the Chinese systems, was communism.

This book takes the view (which is open to question) that liberal democracy is generally more conducive to human welfare and happiness than communism.

▼ Karl Marx, the German philosopher who foretold the eventual collapse of capitalism while an exile in Britain, the cradle of the liberal capitalist system.

KARL MARX

Modern communism (sometimes called 'socialism') was the brainchild of the German thinker Karl Marx (1818-83). The essence of his theory was that history, like science, operates according to knowable laws. According to these laws, societies move through stages of development, from feudalism, to capitalism and, finally, to communism. Ultimately, the engine that brings about these changes is economics.

Marx said that the capitalist, free market world was doomed. Available wealth would find its way into the hands of fewer and fewer 'capitalists'. Because these capitalists needed profit, the working class (or 'proletariat') earned wages that under-represented the value of their labour. In other words, they were exploited. Eventually and inevitably, they would rise up, overthrow the capitalists and set up a classless, genuinely democratic society in which there was no private property and everyone was treated equally.

REVOLUTION

Marx believed that an interim type of government would be needed after the fall of capitalism. He called this the 'dictatorship of the proletariat'. It would be headed by a band of communists dedicated to weeding out the last remnants of capitalism and class-based thinking.

Marx's theories were first put to the test not in a major industrial country like the USA or Britain but in Russia, a largely agricultural and old-fashioned empire. Led by Vladimir Lenin (1870-1924), a group of Russian communists known as the Bolsheviks seized power in 1917. They defeated all their opponents in a bloody civil war (1918-1921) and proceeded to establish the world's first communist state.

VLADIMIR LENIN 1870-1924

Born Vladimir Ilyich Ulyanov, Lenin was first inspired by the works of Karl Marx at the age of nineteen. His important contribution to Marxist thinking was believing that a society (i.e. Russia's) could pass from feudalism to communism without going through the capitalist stage of development. After seizing power in the revolution of October 1917, he attempted to put his ideas into practice. The result was the Soviet Union's communist system of government that lasted for over seventy years.

▶ The dawn of a brave new world? A Soviet propaganda painting showing Lenin (with tie) amid a crowd of enthusiastic workers in 1917.

9

▲ Guilty or not? A Soviet committee engaged in 'purging' suspected dissidents from the party in 1933. By 1939 hundreds of thousands of supposed enemies of Stalin's regime had been executed or imprisoned in inhumane work camps.

DICTATORSHIP

One of communism's chief weaknesses appeared the moment Lenin seized power: how were the new leaders to be kept in check? Lenin genuinely wished to help ordinary Russians by giving them decent wages, education and health care, but many of his followers were more interested in advancing their own careers. Moreover, Lenin's belief in the righteousness of his cause led him to establish a one-party state in which no opposition was tolerated.

Any hope that the USSR might develop into a communist Utopia was ended in 1928, when Joseph Stalin came to power. A ruthless and paranoid dictator, Stalin ruled the USSR through the communist party until his death in 1953. Before 1941, he enforced five-year modernization plans for Soviet industry. At the same time, he sanctioned the slaughter of millions of innocent peasants and purged the party, the government and the armed forces of anyone he suspected of opposing him. Only after the collapse of the Soviet Union in 1991 did the full extent of his crimes begin to be realized.

RUSSIA AND THE WEST

In 1917, the Bolsheviks had overthrown a cabinet that endorsed the principles of liberal democracy. This turned Western governments against the Bolsheviks from the start, and during the Russian Civil War Britain and several other Western governments sent troops to support the 'White' opponents of the 'Red' communists.

Western-style democracies remained suspicious of the one-party Bolshevik state throughout the 1920s and 30s. The Soviets encouraged this suspicion by supporting revolutionary communist parties in other countries. The USA, communism's leading opponent, did not formally recognize the USSR's existence until 1933, eleven years after its formation.

UNLIKELY ALLIES

The antipathy between the USSR and liberal democracies before 1939 was a sort of pre-Cold War. It was ended not by any sudden warming in relations, but by the practical necessity of joining forces to defeat a mutual peril: Nazi Germany.

In August 1939, to the West's dismay, Germany and the USSR signed a non-aggression pact. This allowed Hitler, previously a bitter opponent of communism, to forget the threat from the east and attack Western Europe. After startling victories in France and the Low Countries, in June 1941 he ripped up the pact and launched a massive assault on Stalin's Russia. For the next four years liberal democracy and communism, the most unlikely of allies, had no choice but to fight together.

JOSEPH STALIN, 1879-1953

Stalin joined the Bolsheviks (Lenin's communist party) long before the 1917 revolution. After Lenin's death in 1924, Stalin used his position as party secretary to isolate and eliminate his rivals. As head of the Soviet state, he modernised the country and led it to victory over the Nazis. He did so, however, at the cost of millions of lives. Modern Russia still bears the scars of his dictatorship, which was arguably the most brutal of modern times.

▼ The pact that shocked the world – Molotov, the USSR's commissar for foreign affairs, signs the Nazi-Soviet Pact in August 1939.

LIBERALS AND CAPITALISTS

The roots of liberal democracy stretch back to the English Revolution of the 17th century. This left a representative parliament as the key element in the English political system. In the next century, the English experience and the ideas of the Enlightenment inspired revolutions in America and France. These two upheavals developed further the principles of liberal democracy.

In a liberal democracy no individual, group or institution is supreme. Where a monarch remains (as in Britain), their position is that of figurehead. Ultimate power is in the hands of the people, who choose their government through elections. Governments make laws, which apply to every citizen alike, including members of the government. The government may be opposed, opposition being expressed mainly through political parties and the media. Parties give electors a choice of policies at election time. Within limits, individuals are free to express their own opinions.

▼ People power – the citizens of Paris storm the Bastille, an ancient royal fortress-prison, at the start of the French Revolution, July 1789.

DEMOCRACY

Both the Western and Soviet governments claimed to believe in democracy, described by Abraham Lincoln as 'government of the people, by the people, for the people'. But whereas Western governments gave priority to government by the people, the Soviets emphasized government for the people.

This difference had important consequences for the way people lived under each system. In the West, with its stress on individual freedom and choice, there was a wide gap between the rich and poor. In the USSR income levels were much closer (though on average lower than in the West) and no one was unemployed. On the other hand, because communism was supposed to be the most 'advanced' form of society, criticism of the government was banned as backward-looking and anti-social.

CAPITALISM AND COMMUNISM

In the USSR all wealth was owned by the state and distributed for the benefit of its citizens. Prices, rents and wages were decided centrally. This got rid of extremes of poverty but hamstrung enterprise. What was the point in working hard if the main beneficiary was the state, particularly when (as in the USSR) that state was widely seen as corrupt?

Western governments, led by the USA, believed in a free enterprise (or 'capitalist') economic system. The market (i.e. what you could get) decided prices and wages. Although all governments regulated the market to some degree, individuals' wealth (or lack of it) depended upon environment and circumstance as well as their own efforts.

▼ The Constitutional Convention held in Philadelphia, Pennsylvania, 1787, signs the newly-drafted US Constitution. The document provided a template for liberal democracy the world over.

FREEDOM OF SPEECH

Central to the Western way of life was the idea of freedom of speech. It was guaranteed in law to Americans, together with other freedoms, in the first Amendment to their constitution, accepted in 1791.

"Congress shall make no law respecting an establishment of religion, or prohibiting the free exercise thereof; or abridging the freedom of speech, or of the press; or of the right of the people peaceably to assemble, and to petition the government for a redress of grievances."

▲ Devastation wrought by Japanese aircraft on US warships in Pearl Harbor, December 1941. The surprise attack finally convinced American public opinion that the US should enter World War II on the side of Britain and its allies.

THE ARSENAL OF DEMOCRACY

When the Nazis invaded the USSR in 1941, Britain, backed by its empire, was the only major liberal democracy still at war with fascism. Germany and Italy, the fascist Axis, had overwhelmed or allied with every European nation apart from neutral Sweden, Switzerland and Spain. The US, though also technically neutral, had since 1940 supported Britain with a 'bridge of ships' across the Atlantic.

President Franklin D. Roosevelt wished America to act as the 'arsenal of democracy'. By the Lend-Lease Act of March 1941, Congress empowered him to provide equipment and supplies to any nation whose defence was thought necessary for American security. The Japanese attack on the US naval base at Pearl Harbor and Germany's declaration of war on the US (December 1941) made Soviet Russia an American ally. Of the $50 billion in Lend-Lease aid provided by 1945, some $11 billion went to the USSR. Military necessity had thus made the US the arsenal of communist as well as liberal democracy.

AMERICA'S PROBLEM

By early 1942, therefore, the US was in a highly complex military and diplomatic position. It was at war with the Axis powers of Germany, Italy and Japan which, by Anti-Comintern Pacts of 1936-7, had declared themselves deeply hostile to communism. As the world's most powerful liberal democracy, the US was also bitterly opposed to communism. But necessity had bound it in alliance with the world's leading communist state, the USSR.

The situation was further complicated by events in China. From the mid-1920s to the mid-1930s, China had been ravaged by a civil war between the Chinese Communist Party

(CCP) and the US-backed Guomindang (Kuomintang or KMT). When war broke out with Japan in 1937, the CCP and the KMT formed a United Front against the invader. The Japanese attack on Pearl Harbor brought the US into alliance with this partly-communist Chinese United Front.

By the autumn of 1943, the Soviet Red Army was driving the Germans out of the USSR, the US and its allies had cleared Axis forces from North Africa and invaded Italy, and the Japanese were on the retreat in the Pacific. With eventual victory now likely, the leaders of the pragmatic alliance turned their minds to the shape of the post-war world. Not surprisingly, their respective visions were very different.

FRANKLIN D. ROOSEVELT 1882-1945

Born into a wealthy New York family, Roosevelt trained as a lawyer before entering politics. He made a name for himself as a reforming Democrat and was elected president in 1932 on the promise of tackling the Great Depression. His measures had some success and his radio 'fireside chats' to the nation brought him immense popularity. He was re-elected in 1936, again in 1940 and yet again in 1944 – a testimony to his outstanding skills as a leader in both peace and war.

▼ "The end of the beginning" (Winston Churchill): British gunners operating during the battle of El Alamein (Oct-Nov 1942), the victory that marked the turning of the tide against the Nazis in World War II.

CHAPTER THREE

Planning for Peace

▲ Charter partners –
Roosevelt (front left) and
Churchill (front right) and
officers of H.M.S. *Prince of Wales*
on which the two premiers
signed the Atlantic Charter on
14 August 1941.

THE ATLANTIC CHARTER

In August 1941, British Prime Minister Winston Churchill and US President Franklin D. Roosevelt met on board a warship off the coast of Newfoundland. Together they produced a blueprint for the post-war world known as the Atlantic Charter.

The Charter set out eight principles. These included the right of people to choose their own government, free trade, no seizure of territory by the warring nations and no territory to change hands without its inhabitants' consent. A new international organization (the future United Nations) was proposed but not included in the Charter. The USSR, reeling under the impact of the Nazi invasion, was one of several nations to express support for the Charter.

THE BIG THREE

The 'Big Three' Allied leaders (Roosevelt, Churchill and Stalin) met together for the first time in Tehran, Iran, in late November 1943. Stalin persuaded his allies to agree to the expansion of the USSR into Polish territory after the war. This suggested that his support for the Atlantic Charter was diplomatic rather than heartfelt.

Churchill showed similar political cynicism when he met Stalin in Moscow in October 1944. The prime minister accepted that Romania and Bulgaria would fall within a Soviet sphere of influence, while Hungary and Yugoslavia would be subject to joint influence. The fate of Poland was left undecided.

YALTA

The Big Three met again at Yalta in the Crimea in February 1945. At Stalin's insistence, the permanent members of the United Nations' Security Council were to have a veto. It was

The Big Three – (left to right) Churchill, Roosevelt and Stalin at the Yalta Conference, February 1945. Roosevelt has sometimes been criticized for taking too soft a line towards Stalin at the conference.

further agreed to divide Germany and Austria into zones occupied by the victorious Allies. Roosevelt and Churchill also accepted, reluctantly, that the USSR could collect $20 billion in war damage reparations from Germany.

Poland was left within the Soviet sphere. Although Stalin promised to let the Poles freely elect their government, Churchill and Roosevelt probably realized he was unlikely to honour the undertaking. The West, eager for Stalin's assistance in the war against Japan, had been forced to accept the inevitable: the USSR now dominated Eastern Europe. Although Roosevelt, by his tact, was able to keep the mood at Yalta harmonious, to some, by the close of the conference, the front lines of the future Cold War were clearly discernible.

WINSTON S. CHURCHILL 1874-1965

After a spell in the army, Churchill made a name for himself as a journalist before entering politics in 1900. His roller-coaster political career, which included two changes of party and several cabinet positions, seemed to have ended by the 1930s. However, when his ferocious warnings about the danger of Nazism proved correct, in May 1940 he became prime minister (aged 65). He immediately recognized the importance of good relations with the United States and made much of his personal friendship with Roosevelt.

A NEW PRESIDENT

Roosevelt was replaced by his vice-president, Harry S. Truman. The change was deeply significant. Roosevelt had always hoped to build the post-war world on the foundation of US-Soviet cooperation, ideally through the United Nations. To this end he had deliberately distanced himself from Churchill so that Stalin would not feel isolated. This strategy may have been unrealistic in the long term, but it had at least kept US-Soviet relations amicable.

Three things can be said about Harry Truman in relation to the start of the Cold War. First, he was woefully ignorant in the field of foreign affairs: Roosevelt and he had had only two private meetings since the 1944 election. Second, Truman had little time for detail. He was a straightforward man who believed that if the Soviets (or anyone else) broke their word, they should be duly reprimanded. Finally, for four years Truman held the ultimate military trump card: the atom bomb.

POTSDAM

The final summit meeting of the Grand Alliance began in Potsdam, Germany, on 17 July 1945. The date was significant: the previous day the US had successfully exploded the first atomic bomb. Truman kept the news from Stalin for several days. The Big Three were represented by Stalin, Truman and, initially, Churchill. Following the latter's defeat in the July general election, his place was taken by the Labour prime minister, Clement Atlee. The change had little impact on the talks. Britain, bankrupt and exhausted, could not challenge the new world order dominated by the two 'superpowers'.

Now Germany had surrendered (9 May), Truman's primary objective was to get Stalin to guarantee that the USSR would enter the war against Japan. This the Soviet leader did, although the commitment was largely superseded by the nuclear destruction of Hiroshima and Nagasaki (6 & 9 August) and Japan's surrender five days later.

▼ New man, old problems. President Truman stands between Stalin and Churchill at the opening of the Potsdam Conference, July 1945. The US President's confident glance towards Stalin suggests that he knew something the Soviet premier did not – that the US had successfully tested an atom bomb.

In Europe Stalin achieved several of his objectives. He agreed to the division of a de-Nazified and de-militarised Germany into zones of occupation from which the USSR could take reparations. The agreement left much of eastern Germany in Soviet hands. The West accepted that Romania, Bulgaria and Hungary also lay within the Soviet sphere. The futures of Poland and Czechoslovakia were less certain, although the Soviet presence in both countries did not bode well for liberal democracy there.

NUCLEAR WEAPONS

Allied scientists employing 120,000 people throughout the USA took three years to develop 'Little Boy', the atomic bomb that destroyed Hiroshima. Although the project – code-named 'Manhattan' – was top secret, it was infiltrated by Soviet spies. The information they obtained enabled the USSR to build its bomb much quicker than the US expected. The power of the hydrogen bomb, which the US first exploded on 1 November 1952, was a thousand times greater than 'Little Boy' and raised the nuclear stakes to horrifying new levels.

◀ The atomic mushroom over Nagasaki, 9 August 1945. The terrifying shadow of 'the bomb' hung over the world for the next forty-five years.

THE POST-WAR WORLD

The Second World War had completely changed the world order. In 1939, Britain and Germany, and to a lesser extent France and Italy, were major powers. The Soviet Union, weakened by Stalin's paranoia, was isolated and inward-looking. Japan challenged European dominion in the Far East. The United States, still recovering from the Great Depression, was internationally uncommitted.

By 1945 Japan, Germany, France and Italy were in ruins. Britain, although it had not been invaded and had lost only 330,000 lives (Germany lost 5.2 million), was in serious decline and negotiating a further $3.75 billion loan from the US to keep going. Into the vacuum created by the collapse of the former Great Powers stepped the USA and the USSR, both learning to play a major role on the world stage.

▼ The might of the USA – a production line of Douglas Dauntless dive bombers in Long Beach, California stretches as far as the eye can see.

THE SUPERPOWERS

At first glance it might seem obvious that the US would dominate the post-war world. Its economy had doubled during the war, making it by far the greatest industrial power ever seen. In 1945, for example, it had manufactured almost 50,000 aircraft (USSR, 21,000; Britain, 12,000) and 1,500 warships (USSR, 11; Britain, 64). The Allied victory had been made possible by American money and its 11.5 million troops. The US also possessed nuclear weapons.

By comparison the USSR was in a bad way. It had lost perhaps 27 million lives. 32,000 factories, over 71,000 towns and villages and 100,000 farms had been destroyed. Nevertheless, it commanded the largest army ever assembled (over 20 million) and its communist ideology had some appeal in countries impoverished by war. Not surprisingly, Soviet-backed communist parties flourished in Eastern Europe. Communism had sympathetic supporters, too, in Italy, France, Greece and other Western nations. In July 1945, even the British had rejected Churchill's Conservatives in favour of the socialist Labour Party.

Some Soviet advisors suggested the USSR should build on its popularity and adopt a more friendly attitude towards the West. Stalin and his Foreign Minister Molotov would have none of it. They had been angered at the US's immediate ending of Lend-Lease and its refusal to make further loans. Besides, they argued, in 1812, 1914 and 1941 Russia had been brutally attacked from the west and they were determined it should never happen again. Security would not come through fickle friendship but by building a buffer zone of dependent, communist states. Thus the Communist Bloc came into being.

SHATTERED EUROPE

The USSR, Poland and Yugoslavia lost more than 10% of their population during the Second World War. Germany, Austria and Greece lost between 5% and 10%. France, Czechoslovakia, Hungary, the Netherlands and Romania lost between 1% and 5%. Only Britain, Bulgaria, Italy and Belgium lost less than 1%.

COUNTRY	MILITARY DEAD	CIVILIAN DEAD
USSR	14.5M	UNKNOWN (13M?)
POLAND	850,000	5.8M
YUGOSLAVIA	1.7M MILITARY AND CIVILIAN	
GERMANY	2.85M	2.3M
AUSTRIA	380,000	145,000
GREECE	16,000	155,000
FRANCE	210,000	173,000
CZECHOSLOVAKIA	6,500	310,000
HUNGARY	750,000 MILITARY AND CIVILIAN	
ROMANIA	520,000	465,000
NETHERLANDS	13,500	236,300
BRITAIN	271,000	60,000
BELGIUM	9,500	75,000
ITALY	280,000	93,000
BULGARIA	18,500	1,500

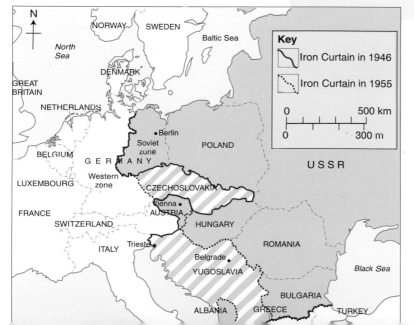

◀ The East-West divide: the changing border, described by Churchill as an 'Iron Curtain', between Soviet-dominated Eastern Europe and the liberal democracies of the West.

ИМПЕРИАЛИЗМ—
ЭТО ВОЙНА!

US

▲ "Imperialism is War!" A Soviet
anti-Western propaganda poster
(1966) that draws on the link,
first made by Lenin, between
capitalism and imperialism.

FALLING TEMPERATURE

As Soviet agents worked to get communists into positions of power throughout Eastern Europe, US anxiety grew. In December 1945 it turned to alarm when pro-Soviet forces threatened to seize part of northern Iran. Although there was yet no Cold War, the temperature was falling fast.

By the end of the year, some of Truman's advisors were starting to think of the USSR not as a former ally but as the enemy. It was probably too late now to prevent the East-West fissure from widening into an unbridgeable chasm.

WHOSE FAULT?

Right-wing commentators have blamed both Stalin and Roosevelt for the coming of the Cold War. The former, they claimed, deliberately rejected collective security and cooperation. He cynically refused to heed the wishes of native populations and set about imposing communism in Soviet-occupied lands. Self-aggrandizement was his motive. Roosevelt was accused of appeasing Stalin. The dictator recognized only brute force, they argued. By acceding to his demands early on, Roosevelt had condemned millions to years of future tyranny.

Left-wingers have been more inclined to blame Truman for the breakdown in East-West relations. They accused him of tactlessness and failing to understand Soviet fears after the horrendous devastation of the war. They also argued that Soviet defensiveness was a response to America's aggressive capitalism. By 1945 the US had captured a huge share of world trade, increasing Soviet fears of American 'economic imperialism'. These fears could have been allayed, it is suggested, had the US appeared more generous by not immediately ending Lend-Lease to the USSR after the war.

Whatever attitude one takes, the Cold War cannot be explained simply in terms of personal failings. First, as we have seen, the US and the USSR endorsed wholly different and conflicting ideologies. Since neither was prepared to accept the merits of the other, harmonious co-existence was difficult to imagine. Second, the superpowers made mistakes because they were relatively inexperienced in global diplomacy. They failed to draw up concrete peace plans during the war, nor did they make satisfactory peace treaties after it. Third, as the US and the USSR had been forced into war by undeclared attack, they remained deeply mistrustful of potential enemies. Finally, the lop-sided military balance (USSR: massive conventional land forces; US: sea and air superiority and nuclear weapons) created a bleak background of mutual suspicion and hostility.

HARRY S. TRUMAN
1884-1972

Truman worked his way from farmworker, soldier and failed shopkeeper to become a US senator in 1935 and Roosevelt's vice-president nine years later. When he became president in 1945, he had little experience in foreign affairs. He relied heavily upon his advisors and his strong sense of personal integrity. Although the latter made Truman less flexible than Roosevelt and may have hastened the East-West rift, it provided the US with firm leadership during the perilous early years of the Cold War.

▶ Harry S. Truman, the US president who in 1947 pledged US support for 'free peoples' in the face of what he perceived to be the advance of communist totalitarianism.

CHAPTER FOUR

Deep Freeze, 1946-47

▲ The communist leader, Josip Tito (extreme right), with a band of his Partisan Army of National Liberation, which fought a successful guerrilla campaign against the Germans during World War Two.

THE COMMUNIST ADVANCE

In 1946, former anti-Nazi guerrillas forcibly established communist governments in Albania and Yugoslavia without Moscow's direct support. However, both soon came under Stalin's influence, although in the case of Marshal Tito's Yugoslavia this lasted only until 1948.

As there was no definitive agreement over Germany and Austria, each remained divided into zones occupied by the US, USSR, Britain and France. Stalinists were installed in the Soviet zones. Elsewhere in Europe, the Soviets set about gaining complete control over other areas within their sphere of influence. Western journalists were prevented from reporting on events behind the Iron Curtain.

SOVIET DOMINATION

Aware that too obvious intervention would alienate the local population and anger the West, Soviet tactics combined caution with ruthlessness. First, exiles returning from the USSR or freed communist prisoners (for example, Gheorghiu-Dej in Romania) were placed in key government positions, such as minister of justice or the interior. This gave them control over the police and security services.

The next step was to remove or discredit influential opponents in politics, the media and elsewhere. This was done by threats, false imprisonment, kidnap and even

THE SOVIET VIEW

In 1946, Nikolai Novikov, the Soviet ambassador in Washington, was putting a very different interpretation on events in Eastern Europe:

"Soviet armed forces are… on the territory of Germany and other formerly hostile countries, thus guaranteeing that these countries will not… again… attack… the USSR. In Bulgaria, Finland, Hungary, and Romania, democratic reconstruction has established regimes that… maintain friendly relations with the USSR. … Poland, Czechoslovakia, and Yugoslavia [also have] democratic regimes… that maintain relations with the USSR on the basis of… friendship and mutual assistance."

murder. Meanwhile, massive pro-communist propaganda campaigns were run. Finally, the state was declared a communist republic, sometimes after elections which the communists were bound to win. Once Soviet-backed communists were in power, they were there for good.

THE TRIUMPH OF TERROR

In Bulgaria a communist-inspired coup had seized power in 1944. Under the Soviet-backed Dimitrov, the country became a communist republic in 1946. The story was similar in Romania, where Moscow backed a government that eliminated the opposition, drove out King Michael and declared the country a Communist People's Republic in 1948. The West took a closer interest in Poland, where Stalin had agreed to free elections. By the time they were held, in January 1947, the opposition had been so weakened that the communists won 80% of the vote.

Previously, the Soviets had allowed elections in Hungary and Czechoslovakia before the communists had established themselves. In November 1945, only 17% of Hungarians voted communist. By 1949, however, terror tactics had transformed the country into a communist republic. 38% of Czechs voted communist in May 1946 and the party declined in popularity thereafter. Then, in 1948, under the communist leader Gottwald, Czechoslovakia became a one-party state of the type prevalent throughout Eastern Europe (see page 38).

25

George F. Kennan in 1952. Six years earlier his 'Long Telegram' from Moscow inspired the White House to take a much firmer line with the USSR, so building up tension and misunderstanding that fostered the Cold War.

WAR OF WORDS

While Moscow was cementing its hold over Eastern Europe, relations between Washington and Moscow were deteriorating fast. Interestingly, as often happened during the Cold War, the change was owed as much to words as deeds.

In February 1946, Stalin made a speech in which he repeated the Marxist belief that capitalism tended to produce wars. There was nothing new in this – communist doctrine had always been that capitalists would use any means, including war, to increase their share of world markets. But a remark that might normally have been dismissed as merely tactless was regarded by Truman's White House as dangerously provocative. Was Stalin suggesting that war between the US and the USSR was inevitable? To learn more, the US government asked George Kennan, an expert in its Moscow embassy, for an analysis of Stalin's foreign policy.

Kennan replied with an 8,000-word telegram that influenced the thinking of American administrations for years. It claimed, rightly or wrongly, that Russia knew only one type of leadership – tyranny. Its rulers, past and present, were terrified of outside influence on their country and would take any step to combat it. The USSR would not feel secure, therefore, until it had removed the threat of the liberal democracies.

CONTAINMENT

The 'Long Telegram', as Kennan's message came to be known, was widely accepted in Washington. Those who disagreed with its thesis no longer had the president's ear. It was time to get tough with the Soviets, Truman decided. The USSR was like a cancer in the body, eating up the healthy tissue around it. To prevent disaster it had to be contained – and the only power capable of doing that was the USA.

Stalin, of course, knew none of this. But he got a good idea of what at least one influential Westerner was thinking when, on 5 March 1946, Winston Churchill repeated to an audience at Westminster College, Fulton, Missouri, his belief that an 'iron curtain' had descended across Europe. Even in the West many thought the remark was going too far. In the USSR they were furious. Churchill, who only nine months previously had been heralded as a staunch ally, was condemned as a warmonger, a racist, a second Hitler. If one needs a specific point at which the Cold War began, then this was it.

THE LONG TELEGRAM

Kennan's statement painted what he believed was Soviet policy in the darkest of colours. For example, he said that Soviet leaders believed,

"A. Everything must be done to advance… strength of USSR… in international society. Conversely, no opportunity must be missed to reduce strength and influence… of capitalist powers.

B. Soviet efforts… must be directed toward deepening and exploiting of differences… between capitalist powers. If these eventually deepen into an "imperialist" war, this… must be turned into revolutionary upheavals within… capitalist countries."

▼ Winston Churchill at Fulton, Missouri, where he made his famous 'Iron Curtain' speech in March 1946.

GETTING TOUGH

The US first got tough over Iran. To prevent Nazi access to the country's oil fields, British and Soviet forces had occupied Iran for the duration of the war. By March 1946 the British had withdrawn, as agreed, but the Soviets lingered on. Washington informed Moscow that the deployment of its troops broke a clear agreement, and might possibly lead to war.

This was the first major Cold War confrontation to come before the newly-formed United Nations (UN). The outcome set a double precedent. First, after face-saving talks, Stalin withdrew his troops. The USSR repeated this tactic – pushing the West to the limit but always stopping short of war – many times during the Cold War.

POWER OF VETO

The second precedent set by the Iran affair concerned the UN. The Security Council had been designed as the UN's main executive body, with the power to enforce decisions with military action. It comprised five permanent members (US,

▼ Shades of deception – Soviet ambassador to the United Nations Andrei Gromyko denies that his country was behind the formation of a communist government in Czechoslovakia in 1948.

USSR, Britain, France and China) and ten elected members. As we saw on page 16, to prevent the West out-voting the USSR, Stalin had insisted that each permanent member had a veto.

The veto rendered the Council impotent without US-Soviet cooperation. When US Secretary of State Byrnes used the Security Council publicly to attack Soviet behaviour in Iran, the Soviet representative Andrei Gromyko simply walked out. The issue, like many to come, was settled not by the international community but by politicians in Washington and Moscow.

'STAYING HERE'

The US soon gave further demonstrations of its new resolution. In May 1946 it banned the USSR from collecting reparations from the US-occupied part of Germany. At a Peace Conference held in Paris it resisted Soviet demands (supported by the French) that Germany be permanently partitioned. When it was clear the issue would not be resolved, Byrnes announced that US forces would remain in Germany. "We will not shirk our duty," he told an audience in Stuttgart in the US zone. "We are staying here."

Later, attention shifted to Turkey. Moscow said its Black Sea Fleet should be free to sail through the Dardanelles into the Mediterranean. When the Turks kept the Dardanelles closed, Soviet troops massed on the Turkish border. The US responded by sending warships to Istanbul – and the Black Sea Fleet stayed where it was.

▲ US Secretary of State James F. Byrnes, shown here signing President Truman's official declaration that the Second World War was over, was a key figure in his administration's decision to maintain a US military presence in Europe.

STANDING FIRM

The Iranian crisis centred around the Tudeh, a Soviet-backed Azerbaijani independence party. When the USSR allowed the Iranian troops into Azerbaijan, the US ambassador in Tehran, George Allen, told Under-secretary of State Dean Acheson why he thought the US had had its way:

"In the Iranian view the quick collapse of the Tudeh Party was due to the conviction of everyone – the Russians, the Iranians, and the Azerbaijanis – that the United States was not bluffing but solidly supporting Iranian sovereignty." He concluded: *"Iran is no stronger than the UN and the UN, in the last analysis, is no stronger than the US."*

▲ One man, one vote – Stalin and Molotov cast their votes in the election for the Supreme Soviet, February 1947. The election in this constituency was won by V.I. Dikushin, the only candidate permitted to stand.

STALIN'S RESPONSE

Churchill's 'Iron Curtain' speech drew an immediate response from Stalin, who, in an interview he gave to the Soviet newspaper *Pravda*, once again emphasized the USSR's defensive policies:

"[Is it surprising that] the Soviet Union, in a desire to ensure its security… , tries to [ensure that Eastern Europe] should have governments whose relations to the Soviet Union are loyal? How can one… qualify these peaceful aspirations of the USSR as 'expansionist tendencies'?… Communism… grew because during the hard years of… fascism in Europe, Communists showed themselves to be reliable, daring and self-sacrificing fighters… for the liberty of peoples."

STALIN'S MOTIVES

By January 1947, the Soviets had twice backed off in the face of US pressure. There are two explanations for this. One is that Stalin was avoiding a war he could not win. By 1948 the US had exploded numerous nuclear weapons. These were not just tests but warnings that war with the US would mean the destruction of many Soviet cities. In such circumstances even so entrenched a dictator as Stalin would almost certainly have fallen.

A second, equally plausible reason why Stalin climbed down is that he never intended to go to war in the first place. Certainly, there is no evidence that he planned to attack the West. His sabre rattling was meant to scare off the Americans rather than threaten them. If this was so, then Kennan's worry (see page 27) that Stalin hoped to destroy capitalism by force was mistaken. In which case, the US policy of 'containing' Soviet expansion was probably also somewhat misguided.

THE CIRCLE OF FEAR

The unhappy conclusion is that the Cold War was primarily the product of fear. Stalin feared the economic and nuclear might of the West; he feared, as always, for his own position; and he feared lest a reunited and revived Germany, supported by its new friends, attack Russia yet again. In response, he acted ruthlessly to surround the Soviet Union with a shield of subservient states.

The US and their allies noted Stalin's aggression and took at its face value his talk of communist world domination. Frightened, they responded with a policy of vigorous containment of the USSR. This fed Stalin's fears further, prompting him to adopt a still more aggressive stance. The result was a vicious circle of fear and misunderstanding which neither side felt confident enough to break.

BRITISH WITHDRAWAL

The next stage in Cold War escalation was not triggered by American or Soviet aggression but by British weakness. Faced with a catastrophic economic crisis, in early 1947 Britain's Labour government decided to cut back immediately on its overseas commitments. It would grant India independence as swiftly as possible, withdraw from Palestine and cut all aid to Greece and Turkey.

Washington reacted immediately, determined that they, and not the Soviets, would fill the power vacuum created by British withdrawal.

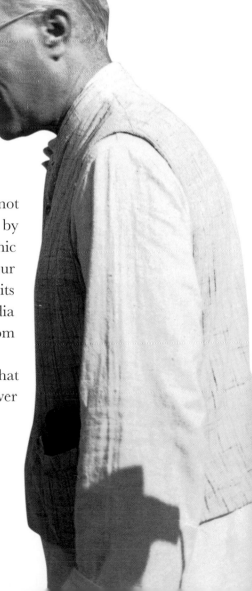

▷ Leader of the world's largest democracy – Jawaharlal Nehru, India's first freely-elected prime minister, in August 1947. During the Second World War, although sympathetic to the Allied cause, he had refused to cooperate with Britain.

31

Containment and Succour

DEMOCRATS AND REPUBLICANS

Unlike Stalin, President Truman was not free to come up with policy and implement it as he wished. The US Constitution carefully divides the power of the federal (central) government between the president and Congress. The latter, for example, declares war, but the president commands the armed forces. More significantly, Congress raises taxation and allocates spending. In other words, a president needs Congress' approval to fund his policies. This, in February 1947, was Truman's problem.

Truman belonged to the Democratic Party. In the November 1946 elections his opponents, the Republicans, had won control of both houses of Congress (the House of Representatives and the Senate) for the first time since 1928. The mood in Congress was conservative, reflecting the nation's wish to get back to normal now the war was over. In traditional American thinking 'normal' meant putting its own

▼ From world war to civil war – members of Greece's communist-controlled National Liberation Front (EAM), an anti-Nazi resistance movement, refused to disarm after German withdrawal. The picture shows EAM prisoners being led away to gaol, 1944.

house in order and leaving the Old World to sort itself out as best it could, just as had happened in 1918. Republicans wanted to 'bring the boys (US troops overseas) home'.

THE ROTTEN APPLE

The news of Britain's plans for an immediate cessation of aid to Greece and Turkey ran through the White House like an electric shock. Turkey, lying along the south-west border of the USSR, was the strategic key to the Middle East, with its vital oil reserves. In Greece a civil war was raging between Tito-backed communists (which the US believed, wrongly, were being supported by Moscow) and pro-Westerners led by the king. Both countries, Washington decided, had to be kept within the Western sphere of influence. But first the Republican Congress had to be persuaded to fund further American overseas commitments.

Truman, accompanied by his new secretary of state, the upright and plain-speaking George C. Marshall, and Under-secretary of State Dean Acheson, invited Congressional leaders to a meeting in the White House on 28 February 1947. At a vital moment in the discussions, Acheson used the 'apple barrel' image: if the communists won control of Greece, he explained, the corruption would spread from this one rotten apple eastwards to Iran and beyond, south into the Middle East and Africa, and west into Italy and France. If this were allowed to happen, before long the Americas would stand alone against a communist world bent on their ruin. His audience was totally convinced.

▲ President Truman presents the Distinguished Service Medal to General George C. Marshall. The general served as US secretary of state from 1947-49 and is remembered in the Marshall Plan of aid to Western Europe.

MIKHAILOVICH MOLOTOV, (1890-1986)

An ally of Stalin since Tsarist times, Molotov (born Skriabin) played a key role in Soviet foreign affairs from 1939 to 1949. He negotiated the Non-aggression Pact with the Nazis (1939), the alliance with Britain (1942) and stood at Stalin's side at Tehran, Yalta and Potsdam. After the war he organized the pacts that bound the states of Eastern Europe to the USSR, so welding closed the Iron Curtain. He was uncompromising over Germany and became famous for saying 'no' to countless United Nations' proposals.

The President speaks. Truman addressing Congress in March 1947, setting out the terms of what became known as the 'Truman Doctrine' by which the US undertook not to withdraw into pre-war isolation.

CONGRESS LISTENS

On 12 March 1947, Truman appeared before Congress and asked for $400 million in aid for Greece and Turkey. It was a moment of great drama. The president, a powerful speaker, put his argument in the plainest possible terms. He presented the US as the champion of freedom against oppression, democracy against tyranny. It was simply a question of good versus evil.

Truman reminded his audience what had happened when America shirked its international responsibilities after the First World War, allowing fascism and communism to flourish; he declared it the country's moral duty to take over active leadership of the free world; he hoped US money would be made available to combat poverty overseas, for "the seeds of totalitarian regimes... spread and grow in the evil soil of poverty and strife"; and he proclaimed that by supporting "free peoples" everywhere, the US would both prevent future conflict and, in time, boost the international capitalist system on which America's prosperity depended. Communism must go "no farther".

THE TRUMAN DOCTRINE

When Truman appeared before Congress on 12 March 1947 to ask for aid for Greece and Turkey, he also outlined his view of the Cold War world. 'At the present moment... nearly every nation must choose between alternative ways of life...

"One... is based upon the will of the majority, and is distinguished by free institutions, representative government, [and]... freedom of speech.

The second... is based upon the will of a minority forcibly imposed upon the majority. It relies upon terror and oppression."

THE TRUMAN DOCTRINE

Truman won the day and Congress voted the aid he requested. The acceptance of what is known as the 'Truman Doctrine' (which some evidence suggests had been under preparation for some time) marked a major turning point in American foreign policy. In a sense it confirmed the role that the US had been edging towards since the end of the war. But there was no guarantee that active US intervention in Europe and elsewhere would have continued. Public opinion had kept America out of the war for two years and, despite growing hostility towards the USSR, there were plenty of signs that by early 1947 Americans had had enough of foreign adventures.

Now, led by their president, Congress and many in the media, Americans were being asked to think again. The free world, they were told, needed them. They responded to the challenge – real or imaginary – and the Truman Doctrine guided America's view of the rest of the world for at least the next twenty-five years.

Washington was now committed to two things: assisting all 'free peoples… resisting attempted subjugation by armed minorities or by outside pressures' (Truman), and containing communism behind its iron curtain. Greece and Turkey were the first states to benefit. In other, more powerful countries, however, the need for American help was almost as pressing.

▼ Dollar power: US aid, suitably draped in the stars and stripes so that it was quite clear where it had come from, arrives in Greece in August 1947.

THE CONDITION OF EUROPE

The parlous situation in post-war Europe is difficult to overstate. The war had cost more than all the continent's previous wars added together. Some 30 million people had been killed and perhaps 60 million driven from their homes.

In 1945 about 23% of Europe's agricultural land was unused. German industrial production had fallen to about 15% of its pre-war level. The French and Italian transport systems were in ruins. The continent was a vast wasteland of shattered homes, shops, factories, roads, railways, bridges and even entire cities. Recovery was painfully slow, in some places non-existent.

Europe provided ample evidence for Truman's belief that misery was the breeding ground of anti-Western regimes. Half Europe was already communist. Czechoslovakia was the only iron curtain country without a communist government. The popularity of the French communist party appeared to be undermining the newly-established Fourth Republic. The Italian communist party, the largest outside Eastern Europe, had a chance of

▼ The ruins of Monte Cassino, Italy, which had witnessed some of the bitterest and most destructive fighting of the Second World War. Similar scenes were common throughout Europe in 1945-6.

winning the elections scheduled for April 1948. To enable its concept of freedom to survive, America had not only to keep its forces in Europe, it needed to help the continent grow rich again. The man who saw this most clearly was US Secretary of State George C. Marshall.

THE MARSHALL PLAN

Marshall announced his European Recovery Program (the Marshall Plan) in a speech at Harvard University on 5 June 1947. Initially $17 billion of aid was proposed (a figure provided by the Conference on European Economic Cooperation). It would be a combination of loans and grants, many in the form of food and machinery.

▲ Funding the German miracle – the poster reads, "It's making progress – with the Marshall Plan" around the words, 'Building work'.

Every European country was invited to apply. Moscow showed some interest at first but when Stalin learned of US plans to rebuild Germany, he condemned the Program as a capitalist plot. He responded by setting up the Communist Bureau of Information (Cominform) as an anti-Western alliance of communist parties. When the Poles and Czechs showed interest in Marshall aid, Stalin threatened to use force against them and they backed off. No other Soviet Bloc country applied.

The size of the aid package alarmed Congress. Although it voted small grants, protracted negotiations delayed approval of the main package into 1948. Was the White House sure the communist threat was as real as imagined? asked the Program's opponents. In February 1948 they got their answer: the communist minority took over Czechoslovakia.

POLITICAL AID

Under-secretary of State Dean Acheson announced what became known as the Marshall Plan in a speech in May 1947. It was widely reported in Europe but not in the US. Its restatement by Secretary of State Marshall a month later, emphasising the Plan's political aim, received widespread coverage on both sides of the Atlantic.

"Our policy is directed against hunger, poverty, despair and chaos. Its purpose should be the revival of a working economy in the world so as to permit the growth of conditions in which free governments can exist."

▲ Czechoslovakia's new communist prime minister, Klement Gottwald, reviews a parade of armed militia in February 1948. The communist takeover in Czechoslovakia was partly the result of US inflexibility.

CZECHOSLOVAKIA

The Czech coalition government formed after the May 1946 elections included communists, but not in a majority. President Benes and Foreign Minister Masaryk tried to steer a middle course between East and West. They were bitterly disappointed, therefore, when Stalin's threats forced them to cancel their application for Marshall Aid. Later, Masaryk approached the US for food to help his country through the hard winter of 1947-8. Washington unwisely rejected the request on the grounds of his seemingly anti-American stance. Stalin immediately offered Czechoslovakia 600,000 tons of grain.

In February 1948 the non-communist members of the Czech government resigned. They hoped Benes would call fresh elections in which the communists would be routed. But faced with communist-organized rallies, Benes lost his nerve and asked the communist leader Gottwald to form a provisional government. When elections were held in May, only communists were permitted to stand. The iron curtain remained closed about Czechoslovakia for the next forty years.

THE LIFELINE

The White House used the communist takeover in Czechoslovakia to whip up anti-Soviet fervour. The frightened Congress approved $5.3 billion of aid for Europe almost immediately. More followed over the next four years until the total had reached over $13 billion.

The British Foreign Secretary Ernest Bevin described Marshall Aid as a "lifeline to a drowning man". Although economists nowadays disagree exactly how important a part the aid played in Europe's recovery, all countries certainly benefited. In some – Greece, for example – US help was vital. Marshall's programme also boosted the American economy.

The US government bought food aid from US farms. Aid in the form of machinery, such as tractors and lathes, came from American manufacturers. Even the cash given as grants and loans benefited the donor because much of it was spent on goods only available in the US.

The political consequences of the Marshall Plan were as important as the economic ones. It accelerated and hardened the division of the continent by forcing countries to decide where they stood. France and Italy were brought firmly into the Western sphere, while Czechoslovakia, Poland, Yugoslavia and Finland remained outside. In Western Europe the business of organizing Marshall Aid sowed seeds of cooperation that grew into the European Economic Community and, eventually, into the European Union.

PEACE-MONGERING

▲ An American cartoon of 1947 suggesting how Marshall Aid would keep Western Europe outside the Soviet sphere of influence.

MARSHALL AID

This graph (not to scale) shows that the scale of Marshall Aid was massive – the modern equivalent of almost $140 billion. To avoid the problem of European debt, which had crippled the continent after World War I, eighty per cent of the money was given as grants.

MARSHALL PLAN AID TO WESTERN EUROPE

$3.2b — UK
$2.7b — France
$1.5b — Italy
$1.4b — West Germany
$1.1b — Netherlands
$694m — Greece
$677m — Austria
$566m — Belg/Lux
$271m — Denmark
$254m — Norway
$221m — Turkey
$146m — Ireland
$107m — Sweden
$50m — Portugal
$32m — Trieste
$29m — Iceland

CRISIS AT BERLIN

At Yalta, Potsdam and Paris the Allies had failed to agree a final settlement for Germany (see page 17). However, they had accepted three intermediate developments. First, land to the east of the Oder and Neisse rivers should be given to Poland. Second, Germany to the west of this line should be divided into Russian, American and British zones of occupation. (The French later insisted on, and occupied, a fourth zone.) Third, Germany should be demilitarized, denazified and democratized ('the three Ds').

WHOSE DEMOCRACY?

Over denazification there was full agreement. But demilitarization caused problems and over democratization there was no agreement whatsoever. To the West it meant establishing Germany as a liberal democracy supported by a thriving capitalist economy. To the USSR it meant installing a Soviet-style communist government and a tightly controlled economy. The two approaches were incompatible.

The first clash had come in May 1946, when the USA stopped the USSR collecting reparation payments from its zone. The Soviets were further annoyed in September when Truman had announced that US forces were remaining in Germany for the foreseeable future. Relations over Germany worsened further when, in January 1947, the US and British zones were united to form 'Bizonia'. The French zone made it 'Trizonia' in March 1948. Boosted by talented refugees from the east and Marshall Plan aid, the western zones recovered fast.

A DIVIDED CITY

Attention now focused on Berlin, deep within the Soviet zone. The capital city was divided like the rest of Germany into

▼ Germany after the war, showing the zones of occupation and the three vital air corridors between Berlin and the West.

Key
Areas occupied by:
☐ U S S R
☐ Britain
☐ United States
☐ France

Soviet, US, British and French sectors. Understandably, Stalin feared the armed, capitalist enclave behind the Iron Curtain and wished to see it removed.

In June 1947 Berliners elected an anti-communist mayor, Ernst Reuter. His authority was immediately denied in the Soviet sector. The following February the Western powers met in private to discuss Germany's future. Angry at being left out, the USSR left the Allied Control Council that supervised German affairs.

Matters came to a head in June 1948 when the Western powers agreed to replace the old Reichsmark in Trizonia (including Berlin) with a new Deutschmark. The USSR objected and stepped up its harassment of road, rail and canal links with West Berlin. The West refused to back down and by August the harassment had become a total blockade. 2.5 million West Berliners faced starvation within weeks.

▲ Tempelhof, one of West Berlin's three airports which from August 1948 were the sector's only links with the outside world.

RUSSIA'S FEARS

Marshal Zhukov, writing to Stalin on 24th May 1946 from Berlin, advises the Soviet government to reject an American draft treaty for the demilitarisation of Germany. The letter shows how, less than a year after the end of the war, a chasm of suspicion and mistrust had opened between the former allies.

"Workers of the world, Unite!

In my view the real purpose of the draft treaty is:

- *a wish to end the occupation of Germany and to get Soviet forces out of there as quickly as possible...;*

- *a wish to hinder sending... reparations from Germany to the USSR;*

- *a wish to keep Germany as a base for future aggression against us."*

41

German 'rubble-women', earning 1.20DM an hour and a hot meal every shift, help build a new airport for West Berlin at Tegel, August 1948.

AIRLIFT

On June 24 the Soviets announced that Berlin's four-power administration was over and the Allies had no right to be there. The intention was clear: the enclave of West Berlin was to be eliminated by starvation.

West Berlin was of little strategic value to the Allies. Nevertheless, the Soviet threat was a real challenge to the Truman Doctrine and US resolve. Their response to the blockade, therefore, was immediate and vigorous.

On June 26 the US and Britain began an 'airlift', flying in food, fuel and other vital supplies to the city from outside. Returning planes carried refugees and industrial exports to the west. For eleven months hundreds of aircraft shuttled back and forth along the three 265-mile air corridors that linked Berlin to western Germany. At the height of the airlift there were always at least thirty aircraft in the air at the same time. Thanks to the 2.3 million tonnes of supplies brought in by the planes, West Berlin managed to survive.

During the airlift, both sides built up their forces as if preparing for war. By mid-July the Soviets had forty divisions in Germany. The Allies had only eight, but they were backed by US strategic bombers, purportedly armed with atomic bombs. It was the first classic Cold War stand-off: posture and threat but no actual conflict.

STALIN RELENTS

The Soviets dared not attack the Allied supply planes for fear of sparking war. Moreover, they were frustrated by Allied disruption of East German communications and hurt by a Western embargo on exports from the Eastern bloc. So, on 12 May 1949, they accepted the inevitable and lifted the blockade. Fearing it might be re-imposed, the Allies continued to stockpile supplies in West Berlin for another four months.

The Berlin blockade was the first great crisis of the Cold War. It confirmed the East-West rift and America's military commitment in Europe. It also altered the way the Western media portrayed Germany: West Germans were now friends and allies, while East Germans and Russians were the new villains. This division became political reality with the creation of the pro-Western German Federal Republic in September 1949 and the Soviet-dominated German Democratic Republic in October.

THE BERLIN AIRLIFT IN DETAIL

★ DURATION: 24 JUNE 1948 TO 12 MAY 1949

★ NUMBER OF FLIGHTS (US): 189,963

★ NUMBER OF FLIGHTS (GB): 87,841

★ NUMBER OF FLIGHTS (FRANCE): 424

★ NUMBER OF PASSENGERS BROUGHT IN: 61,100

★ NUMBER OF PASSENGERS TAKEN OUT: 167,900

★ TOTAL COST: $224,000,000

★ WEIGHT OF SUPPLIES BROUGHT IN: 2,323,738 TONNES

★ WEIGHT OF EXPORTS TRANSPORTED TO THE WEST: 2,500 TONNES

★ CASUALTIES (US): 31

★ CASUALTIES (GB): 39

▼ A crowd of West Berliners watches anxiously as an American plane comes in to land with a cargo of vital supplies. At the height of the airlift a plane was taking off and landing in West Berlin every 90 seconds.

CHAPTER SIX

Hot War

PREPARATIONS FOR WAR

By the time of the Berlin crisis, there was a real possibility that US-Soviet hostility would boil over into war. Washington took various steps designed to deter such an eventuality and, if these failed, to win the consequent war.

In 1947 the US had reorganised its armed forces under Joint Chiefs of Staff and a Secretary of Defence. The National Military Establishment Act combined the War and Navy Departments, made the Air Force a separate entity and gave the Strategic Air Command responsibility for planes carrying atomic bombs. In 1948, sixty of these bombers, B-29 Superfortresses, were flown to bases in Britain. They were not armed with atomic weapons, though this was not widely known.

In 1949, at the height of the Berlin crisis, Truman announced that the US was sending military aid to Western Europe. Three months later, the US, Canada, Britain and nine

▼ The might of America: massed ranks of Boeing B17s, 'Flying Fortresses', on a raid over Japan during the Second World War. Before the advent of the long-range missile, the bomber was the US's principal offensive weapon and the only way of delivering nuclear weapons.

other European nations signed a treaty setting up the North Atlantic Treaty Organization (NATO). The treaty bound them to come to each other's aid if attacked. The message from a united West to the USSR was clear: hands off.

Meanwhile, the Soviet Union had been pressing ahead with the development of its own nuclear weapons. In August 1949 its first A-bomb was tested in secret. The West learned about it when increased radiation was detected. The impact of the discovery was immediate and dramatic. In military terms the US had lost its Ace of Spades and the age of nuclear terror had begun.

THE CIA

The Central Intelligence Agency was established by the National Security Act (1947) to collect, coordinate and analyse US foreign intelligence. In other words, it became the heart and mind of American espionage and counter-espionage. Under presidential control, it was primarily concerned with infiltrating the Soviet system to get advance warning of Soviet technological advances, military deployment and political initiatives. At first its activities were promoted as a super effective defence of the 'free world', but when the CIA came under widespread public scrutiny in the mid-1960s its reputation was severely tarnished.

CHINA

The news coming out of China did little to lighten Washington's gloom. Not long after Japan's surrender, the CCP and KMT had resumed their bitter civil war (see page 15). Despite $2 billion of US aid, Chiang Kai-shek's KMT threw away their early advances and by the summer of 1949 the communist forces of Mao Zedong controlled the most populous country on earth.

The 'fall' of China to the communists was a serious blow to the Truman administration. Far from containing communism, it had presided over its massive expansion. (Interestingly, though, Mao had received very little backing from Stalin, who for a long time regarded him as merely a rebellious peasant.) Wherever communism threatened next, therefore, Truman was determined to resist it with all the force he could muster.

▶ Mao Zedong, China's charismatic communist leader whose seizure of power in 1949 had not been widely predicted, even in the USSR.

N

CHINA

USSR

Yalu River

NORTH
KOREA

.Chongju

Sea of Japan

■ Pyongyang

armistice line, 1953

Panmumjom

38th parallel

Inchon\.

■ Seoul

SOUTH
KOREA   Taejon

Yellow Sea

furthest extent
of communist
advance

•Pusan

0   300 km

0   150m

JAPAN

▲ Korea split into
warring countries during
the Korean War, 1950-53.

KOREA DIVIDED

In 1910 Korea had become a Japanese colony. During the Second World War, Koreans were extremely harshly treated by their Japanese masters, and in 1943 the US, Britain and Chiang Kai-shek's China agreed that Korean independence should be an official Allied war aim.

The USSR declared war on Japan on 8 August 1945 and swiftly moved Red Army divisions through Japanese-occupied Manchuria and into northern Korea. The White House, afraid lest the whole of Korea fall into Soviet hands, suggested the country be divided between US and Soviet occupation forces. Since there were no US forces in Korea, this was at best hopeful. Surprisingly, the Kremlin accepted America's proposal and the Red Army duly halted along the 38th parallel. As Korea is not divided from east to west by any natural features, the chosen line of latitude was a wholly artificial frontier. A few weeks later, US forces took up positions south of the new border.

STAND OFF

Although in December 1945 the US and the USSR signed an agreement for administering Korea and returning the country to independence, little progress was made. The situation was similar to partitioned Germany, where each side feared withdrawal would lead to takeover by the other. So the Koreans, who had no wish to live in a divided land, became the latest victims of the escalating Cold War.

Over the next four years North Korea settled down under the Soviet-favoured leader Kim Il Sung, and the South under its US-favoured leader Syngman Rhee. Kim eliminated non-communist opposition and established a socialist economy.

46

DEFENCE SPENDING

The crises of 1949-50 had a dramatic effect on military spending, particularly in the USA. By 1951 America's defence budget was greater than those of every other country added together. As weapons became technologically more sophisticated (and therefore more expensive) year by year, the US's wealth gave it a massive advantage over the Soviet Union.

Large numbers of Koreans fled to the South, where capitalism (and corruption) flourished. Although the north-south border was tense, by the end of June 1949 both Soviet and US forces had been withdrawn, leaving the Koreans to sort out their differences for themselves.

KIM'S REQUEST

Soviet nuclear testing and Mao's triumph in China sharply re-focused US foreign policy. The White House ordered the development of a new type of nuclear weapon, the Hydrogen Bomb. To increase its conventional (non-nuclear) power it requested a five-fold increase in military expenditure to $50 billion.

Meanwhile, Mao and Stalin settled their differences in a Treaty of Friendship, Alliance, and Mutual Assistance (February 1950). This considerably strengthened Stalin's position in Asia, and he began to take seriously Kim's repeated suggestion that the North complete the communist takeover of Korea.

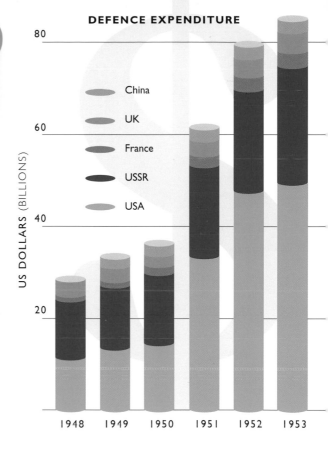

DEFENCE EXPENDITURE

US DOLLARS (BILLIONS)

China
UK
France
USSR
USA

1948 1949 1950 1951 1952 1953

▼ The signing of the Sino-Soviet treaty of friendship in February 1950. The photograph is one of the few to show Stalin and Mao Zedong together (standing back left in idealized poses) – although they may have been added to the picture later for propaganda purposes.

▲ "Remember June 25th, the day the Communists Invaded" – a propaganda poster issued by the government of South Korea.

KIM'S ATTACK

The Korean War began on 25 June 1950 with a massive North Korean attack over the 38th parallel. The 100,000-strong communist army, armed with Soviet weapons and tanks, reached the Southern capital of Seoul in three days. The US immediately sent troops to Rhee's aid, commanded by General Douglas MacArthur, an outspoken World War II veteran. Simultaneously, it urged the United Nations to intervene against North Korean aggression.

The Security Council responded by summoning a UN force to aid the South Koreans. The USSR was boycotting the UN in protest at its exclusion of communist China and therefore unable to use its veto. This left the North Koreans facing the South Koreans, the US and a sixteen-nation UN coalition that eventually included British, Australians, New Zealanders and Turks.

DOUGLAS MACARTHUR (1880-1964)

A brilliant yet controversial soldier and administrator, MacArthur was decorated thirteen times during the First World War and masterminded the Allied advance across the Pacific in the Second. After the war, commanding the Allied forces occupying Japan, he acted virtually as the country's unelected president. This increased his self-importance and sense of mission, leading to his disagreement with the Truman administration and his dismissal in 1951. The next year he failed to be nominated as a candidate for the US presidency.

PUSAN AND INCHON

At first, US forces fared no better than the South Koreans. They were defeated at Taejon and driven south-west to an enclave of territory around Pusan. Here, while US aircraft harried Kim's supply lines, MacArthur gathered his forces behind the Naktong River for a counter-attack.

MacArthur struck on 15 September, combining a frontal assault with the biggest seaborne landing since D-Day at Inchon, 150 miles behind the enemy lines. The offensive was a spectacular success. UN-US forces reached Seoul on 26 September and advanced to the 38th parallel.

STRIKING NORTH

Truman had believed, wrongly, that Kim's offensive was part of a Soviet plan for world domination. (Stalin had simply backed an aggressive ally.) In US eyes, therefore, the operation in South Korea had been simply to 'contain' communism.

The situation had now changed. With MacArthur and Rhee urging pursuit of the retreating North Koreans over the 38th parallel, the temptation to try to reunite Korea under a US-backed government was too great to resist. MacArthur was allowed to advance into the North.

Kim's position was desperate. Stalin, furious at his failure, had withdrawn most Soviet advisors. On 19 October MacArthur captured the Northern capital of Pyongyang and drove towards the Yalu River and the border with China. Here, in late October, the US captured enemy soldiers who did not understand their Korean interrogators. This was hardly surprising – the captives were not Koreans at all, but Chinese.

▼ US marines advancing towards Inchon after their successful seaborne landing behind the enemy lines five days earlier. Technically, the US forces were fighting for the United Nations.

49

ENTER CHINA

Neither Stalin nor Mao wanted to commit forces in Korea. But Mao could not accept US troops on his border and so dropped diplomatic hints that they should withdraw. When the Americans ignored him, he sent 'volunteers' to assist the North Koreans. It was some of these men that the US had captured. The Chinese inflicted a sharp defeat on the coalition, then withdrew.

Mao's message was clear: pull back or face more of the same. However, MacArthur did not believe he had been fighting the Chinese and the US failed to take the hint. On 26 November, Mao responded with a huge attack, commanded by the experienced General Peng De-Huai, that sent the coalition forces reeling backwards.

ADVANCE AND RETREAT

What the Chinese army lacked in airpower and heavy weapons, it made up for in numbers and bravery. The US-UN troops were simply overwhelmed by wave after wave of advancing Chinese.

▼ Communist artillery bombing UN-American positions during the Korean War. North Korean and Chinese offensives rocked the Americans, who initially underestimated their enemies' military capacity.

The communists retook Pyongyang on 6 December and Seoul a month later. In February 1951, the US-UN coalition launched counter-attacks. By late March, they had returned to the 38th parallel where they managed to withstand a huge Chinese counter-offensive.

TO BOMB OR NOT TO BOMB?

China's intervention deeply concerned President Truman, who feared all-out war with China might lead to war with the USSR. He insisted, therefore, that the conflict should remain a limited operation. MacArthur, passionately anti-communist, wanted the US to throw itself wholeheartedly into the war and bomb Chinese cities. In April Truman replaced him with another distinguished World War II veteran, General Matthew B. Ridgeway.

STALEMATE

With the front line stabilized near where the conflict had started, the war had reached stalemate. Tragically, a political solution proved as elusive as a military one. Talks broke down on several occasions, leading to fresh hostilities.

Few gains were made on the ground, where both sides had adopted strong defensive positions. Meanwhile, American bombers pounded Northern supply routes, factories and cities. The weight of bombs dropped on North Korea was only slightly less than that dropped on Germany during the entire Second World War.

A LESSON OF SUPREME IMPORTANCE

The success of Chinese forces in the Korean War took many Western observers by surprise. The delighted Chinese, as this propaganda report of September 1953 shows, said the war should encourage all colonies to fight for independence:

"It is a lesson whose international meaning is of supreme importance. It proves beyond all doubt that the time when a Western aggressor could occupy a country… has gone for ever. It proves that a nation, once aroused, which dares to rise and fight for its glory, its independence, and the safety of the fatherland, is invincible."

▼ Bomber power – devastation and disruption caused by a napalm attack of US B-26 bombers on North Korean supply lines, 1950.

▲ As one soldier to another… President-elect Eisenhower (left, seated), who commanded the Allied forces in Europe in 1944-45, shares rations with US troops in Korea in 1951. Eisenhower talked tough but stopped short of attacking positions within China.

DWIGHT EISENHOWER (1890-1969)

Eisenhower had a remarkable ability to get on with almost everyone he met. He put this to good effect during the Second World War, when he was supreme commander of difficult Allied operations. These included the D-Day landings and the advance into Germany. After the war he commanded the NATO land forces before being elected US president in November 1952. During his two terms of office he showed wise moderation and resisted right-wing demands that America be more aggressive towards communism.

ARMISTICE

In November 1952, the Republican Dwight Eisenhower was elected US president. A careful yet committed anti-communist, he sought to end the war on terms favourable to the US. To this end, in May 1953 he said the US might subject Beijing to a nuclear attack.

Eisenhower's threat was not needed. Stalin had died in March 1953 and the new Soviet administration had already decided to end the war. As Mao Zedong had reached the same conclusion, an armistice was agreed on 27 July 1953. It was based upon a new North-South border running between a demilitarized zone.

THE COST

Neither side had made significant territorial gains. Korea remained a country divided by fear and hatred. Many of its larger towns and cities were in ruins. Perhaps five million of its people had become refugees, most fleeing from the North to the South.

The casualties on both sides, civilian and military, were horrific. Nearly a million North Koreans and perhaps 600,000 South Koreans lost their lives. The Chinese dead may have totalled half a million. 57,000 United Nations' soldiers and airmen were killed, 54,000 of whom were American. A further 100,000 Americans were wounded.

COLD WAR

The Korean war had a major impact on the Cold War. First, it reinforced America's hatred of communism and its mistaken belief that China and the

USSR aimed at world domination. Believing, incorrectly, that the nuclear threat had hastened peace, the US built up its nuclear arsenal. Moreover, after holding back the communists in Korea, it believed it could do the same elsewhere. This was one reason for US military intervention in Vietnam, 1964-75.

Second, the Soviets would never again let the US act under the United Nations' umbrella. This made the UN powerless as a Cold War power broker. Not until 1991, after Soviet communism had collapsed, would the UN again take military action against an aggressor (Iraq).

Third, the war brought Japan firmly into the Western alliance. The billions of dollars the American military spent there acted like Marshall Aid in Europe, boosting the Japanese economy. In time, most of Southeast Asia would benefit from Japan's post-war economic miracle.

Finally, the war damaged the new Sino-Soviet alliance. Stalin had been fully prepared to provide China with all the weapons it needed – as long as it paid for them. Mao was angered by this lack of communist fraternity and relations with his northern neighbour cooled.

▼ US troops advance to the front as South Korean women flee to safety on the other side of the road. America's success in Korea was one reason why it was prepared to get involved in Vietnam twelve years later.

CHAPTER SEVEN

The Balance of Terror

THE PASSING OF STALIN

1953 marked no sharp break in the history of the Cold War. Nevertheless, the death of Stalin and the end of the Korean War did suggest a turning point had been reached. The name Joseph Dzhugashvili adopted for himself – 'Stalin', meaning 'Man of Steel' – was remarkably apt. The control he kept over the USSR and its satellites was vice-like; his attitude towards all perceived enemies of the Soviet Union was unbending. He was the Soviet Tsar, driven by a paranoid fear of enemies within and without to maintain his supreme authority.

More than any other individual, Stalin had been responsible for the failure of Roosevelt and Churchill's dreams of collective responsibility and the drift into Cold War. For sure, the West had played its part in the deterioration of East-West relations, but essentially it had reacted to moves initiated in Moscow. Now Stalin had gone, therefore, there was a chance for his successors to preside over a thaw.

▼ Stalinism at its worst – the remains of some 15,000 Poles slaughtered by the Soviet secret police (NKVD) following the partition of Poland between Germany and the USSR in September 1939.

THE BALANCE OF TERROR ★

POST-KOREA

By the end of the Korean War both sides had tested each other and knew, more or less, where they stood. The US had noted the USSR's reluctance to commit its forces openly outside the Soviet Bloc. For their part, the Soviets realized America was prepared to use armed force (perhaps even nuclear weapons) to resist communist expansion.

The Korean War had also shown that, by sheer weight of numbers, the combined conventional power of China and the USSR could match the West's superior technology. This increased the possibility of the West resorting to nuclear weapons in an all-out East-West war. However, as by the end of 1953 both sides had developed the hydrogen bomb (a significant advance on the A-bombs dropped on Hiroshima and Nagasaki), a balance of terror had been established that only a madman would have dared upset.

▲ Communist Viet Minh troops gather for an attack on the French forces occupying Vietnam in January 1951. France's subsequent defeat and withdrawal led to active US military involvement in the region.

A LITTLE WARMTH

There were signs, too, that by December 1953 other Cold War issues were nearing resolution. The Soviets seemed reconciled to losing influence in Austria, which had been partitioned since 1945. The anti-imperialist forces in Indo-China (Laos, Cambodia and Vietnam) were on the verge of driving out the US-backed French. Finally, Senator McCarthy's fanatical anti-communist witch-hunt was running out of steam (see pages 56 and 57). Even the Americans, it seemed, were coming to realize that there was not a Red under every bed.

'AN INESTIMABLE LOSS'

On hearing of Stalin's death, Mao Zedong sent an open telegram (in the *Beijing People's Daily* newspaper on 7th March 1953) to the USSR expressing his condolences. Behind the expressions of sorrow, however, probably lay some relief at the passing of so grasping an ally.

"It was with boundless grief that the Chinese people, the Chinese government, and I myself learned the news of the passing away of the Chinese people's closest friend and great teacher, Comrade Stalin. This is an inestimable loss, not only for the people of the Soviet Union, but for the Chinese people, for the entire camp of peace and democracy, and for peace-loving people throughout the world."

The Red Scare – Senator Joe McCarthy, leader of the US anti-communist witch-hunt of the early 1950s, shows some of his 'evidence' to the press.

ENEMIES WITHIN

Only a nation seriously anxious about the communist threat could have taken seriously Senator McCarthy's vague, almost hysterical accusations (such as these, which he made in a speech to the Women's Club of Wheeling, West Virginia, in February 1950):

"When a great democracy is destroyed it will not be because of the enemies from outside, but rather because of enemies within. At the end of the war we were the strongest nation on earth and morally the most powerful. Yet… we have failed miserably… because of… traitors. … In my opinion the State Department… is thoroughly infested with communists."

THE ARMS RACE

The Cold War did not end until the collapse of communism in Eastern Europe in 1989-90. Until then the features in place by 1953 remained largely intact. The most obvious of these was a crippling arms race, as each side strove to make sure it kept up with the other.

In 1948 American expenditure on defence was about $11 billion. By 1951 it had risen to near $35 billion and two years later it had soared to over $50 billion. During the same period Soviet expenditure climbed from around $13 billion to $25 billion.

McCARTHYISM

A second feature was the development of mutual hostility, reinforced by propaganda. Soviet citizens were accustomed to attacks on enemies of the state, whether foreign powers or supposed subversives within. In peacetime America, however, it had not been a common phenomenon. The books of left-wing writers were shunned by schools and libraries, while anti-communist works (such as *Animal Farm*, 1945, by the British writer George Orwell) were heartily approved. Hollywood joined the anti-Soviet bandwagon with films like *My Son John* (1952).

The most chilling example of America's anti-communist hysteria was the communist witch-hunt led by Senator McCarthy between 1950 and 1953. In

February 1950 McCarthy claimed he had evidence of fifty-seven active communists working within the US State Department (responsible for foreign affairs). In a series of hearings before the Senate Sub-committee on Investigations, some televised, McCarthy's bullying, anti-intellectual questioning ruined the careers of many able and innocent men. Only in 1954 was he censured for bringing the Senate into disrepute.

Another Cold War feature was waging war at arms' length. The Soviet tactic in Korea – supplying arms and advisors but not committing its own men to the front line (although some Soviet fighter pilots flew MiG fighters) – was later adopted by both West and East in several local conflicts, notably in the Arab-Israeli wars.

SPIES AND NON-ALIGNMENT

As each side tried to discover the other's military plans and secrets, spying had become another enduring aspect of the Cold War. So too was the emergence of non-aligned nations, most notably India, that refused to take sides in the East-West split. Finally, as we have seen (page 48), the Soviet misjudgement before the Korean War meant that henceforward US-Soviet hostility would prevent the United Nations from fulfilling its role as an active peacekeeper.

▶ Weapons of a Soviet assassin-spy handed over to American authorities in 1954: two poison bullet guns hidden in cigarette cases (top right) and a three-barreled electric gun that fired poisoned dum-dum bullets.

THE DANGER PHASE

1946-53 was the Cold War's most dangerous phase. It began with a world confused, disrupted and disorientated. The wartime friendships had gone, blown away by the unseemly scrabbling for position in the new political environment. There were few certainties. There was no guarantee, for example, that the US would not withdraw into isolation, as it had done in 1919.

Gradually, order emerged out of the chaos. But it was a new order, one the world had never seen before. It featured two superpowers wedded to opposing ideologies, armed to the teeth, terrified of each other's ambitions and determined not to lose face. It was a situation ripe for war.

AVOIDING THE DROP

And yet no major war came. The main reason for this was also the reason why the situation was so frightening – nuclear weapons. Until August 1949 the Soviets realized that all-out war would mean the destruction of much of the USSR. After

▼ The city of Hiroshima six months after its destruction by an A-bomb in 1945. Fear of repeating such horrific destruction produced the 'balance of terror' that helped prevent the Cold War from becoming hot.

that date, the horrific possibility of a nuclear holocaust hung over both sides. They both knew that the other side was probably prepared to use nuclear weapons as a very last resort, so each tried not to force the other into a corner from which nuclear attack was the only exit.

For all their aggressive posturing and rhetoric, the strategies of both the US and the USSR were largely defensive: America's first wish was to contain communism, while the Soviet Union's prime aim was to protect itself and its way of life. Stalin's aggression in Eastern Europe, over Berlin and in Korea was intended either to boost his security or to test the USA's resolve.

It was a highly dangerous game, nevertheless, and one that might easily have gone wrong, even by accident. The individual players – Truman, Eisenhower and even Stalin – must take some credit for sticking to the rules. Had a man with the mentality of General MacArthur headed either superpower, the first phase of the Cold War might well have ended disastrously.

▲ Nikita Khrushchev, the Soviet premier who spoke of 'peaceful coexistence' between East and West. He may have saved the world from nuclear destruction by backing down during the Cuban Missile Crisis of 1962.

OUTLOOK UNCERTAIN

So, by the autumn of 1953 a new world order had emerged. The East-West rift remained as broad as ever, but it had been clarified, institutionalized, stabilized. In time, the new Soviet premier, Nikita Khrushchev, would talk of the East and West living in 'peaceful coexistence'. Coexistence, yes. But whether a balance of terror would keep it peaceful remained to be seen.

PEACEFUL CO-EXISTENCE

At a summit conference with President Eisenhower in May 1960, the Soviet premier Nikita Khrushchev took a hostile stance against the US for spying on the Soviet Union. Yet he still held out the prospect of future peaceful co-existence.

"The Soviet government is profoundly convinced that if not this US government, then another, and if not another, then a third, will understand that there is no other solution than peaceful coexistence of the two systems, … capitalist and… socialist. It is either peaceful coexistence, or war, which would spell disaster… ."

Timeline

1937
JULY Japanese invasion of eastern China

1939
AUGUST Nazi-Soviet Non-aggression Pact
SEPTEMBER Outbreak of the Second World War in Europe

1941
JUNE German attack on USSR. Atlantic Charter signed
DECEMBER Japanese attack on Pearl Harbor. USA enters the war

1945
FEBRUARY Yalta Conference
APRIL Death of Roosevelt. Truman president of USA
MAY War in Europe ends
JUNE UN Charter presented

JULY Potsdam Conference
AUGUST A-bomb dropped on Hiroshima. Japan surrenders

1948
FEBRUARY Communists take over in Czechoslovakia

JUNE Berlin blockaded (to May 1949)

1949
APRIL NATO founded
AUGUST Soviets explode nuclear device
OCTOBER Mao Zedong declares People's Republic of China (communist)

1951
APRIL General MacArthur dismissed from command of US forces in Korea

1943

NOVEMBER Tehran Conference

1946

Civil war in China (to 1949)

1947

MARCH Truman Doctrine announced

JUNE Marshall Plan announced

JULY CIA established

AUGUST India independent

SEPTEMBER Cominform set up

DECEMBER Civil war breaks out in Vietnam (to 1954)

1950

JANUARY US authorizes deployment of H-bomb

FEBRUARY Senator MacCarthy begins his anti-communist witch-hunt (to 1953)

FEBRUARY Alliance of USSR and China

JUNE Korean War begins

OCTOBER Chinese enter Korean War

1952

NOVEMBER Eisenhower elected US president

1953

MARCH Death of Stalin

JULY Korean War ends

1991

USSR broken up

Glossary

A-bomb atomic bomb, the simplest form of nuclear weapon

appease make concessions to someone to keep them content

Big Three Roosevelt (USA), Stalin (USSR) and Churchill (UK)

bloc group of countries

CIA The Central Intelligence Agency, established in 1947 to manage America's foreign intelligence operations

coalition political or military partnership

collective responsibility acting together to tackle problems

Cominform Communist Information Bureau to co-ordinate the activities of European communist parties

Congress The United States' law-making body

conservative against change

containment US policy of preventing the spread of communism

conventional weapons traditional or non-nuclear weapons

democracy government with the consent of those governed

embargo blockade or banning of trade

guerrillas irregular soldiers generally fighting with hit-and-run tactics

H-bomb hydrogen bomb; nuclear weapon based on power of nuclear fusion

ideology belief or thinking, as in communist or free-market ideology

imperialism seeking to aquire an empire by force

Iron Curtain imaginary impassable barrier along the border between Eastern and Western Europe during the Cold War

left (wing) favouring socialism or communism

Lend-Lease US policy of granting war aid in return for the use of military bases

liberal believing that a government's first task is to protect individual freedom

Marshall Plan The massive aid package provided by the US to Western Europe after the Second World War

NATO North Atlantic Treaty Organization, a defensive alliance of Western nations established in 1949

non-aggression agreeing not to fight

propaganda information slanted to favour one side over another

purge to cleanse or clear out by force

Red Communist or Soviet

reparations goods or money collected by one country to pay for the damage caused by another

Republic state without a monarch

right (wing) inclined towards conservatism and unrestricted capitalism

secretary of state US official responsible, under the president, for conducting the country's foreign policy

Security Council decision-making body of the United Nations

Soviet Union the USSR

Truman Doctrine America's undertaking to defend peoples whose freedom was threatened

United Nations International organization set up in 1945 to guard world peace and foster international understanding and co-operation

USSR Union of Soviet Socialist Republics, communist Russia's empire in Europe and Asia

Further Information

BOOKS

Jeremy Isaacs & Taylor Downing,
Cold War, Bantam, 1998.

John Lewis Gaddis, *We Now Know:
Rethinking Cold War History*,
OUP, 1997.

Daniel Yergin, *Shattered Peace: the Origins of
the Cold War*, Penguin, 1990.

Simon J. Bell, *The Cold War*,
Arnold, 1997.

Fiona Macdonald & Richard Staton,
The Cold War 1945-1989,
Collins Educational, 1996.

Martin McCauley, *The Origins of the Cold War
1941-1949*, Longman, 1993.

WEBSITES

Just because information is on the web, it
does not mean it is true: anyone can put
anything they want on a website. Reputable
organizations like CNN, the BBC, a
university or a well-known museum have
sites you can trust. Here are three useful
sites to start from:

http://www.coldwar.org

**http://www.fordham.edu/halsall/mod/
modsbook46.html**

http://www.cnn.com/specials/cold.war

Index